Man
Hunting

Also by Cathy Hopkins

Divorce for Beginners
Girl Chasing
Keeping It Up
The Joy of Aromatherapy
The World's Best Light-Bulb Jokes (with Edward Phillips)

Man Hunting

A GIRL'S GUIDE TO THE GAME

CATHY HOPKINS
Cartoons by Gray Jolliffe

HarperCollins*Publishers*

HarperCollins*Publishers*
77–85 Fulham Palace Road,
Hammersmith, London W6 8JB

This paperback edition 1995
3 5 7 9 8 6 4 2

First published in Great Britain by
Angus & Robertson (UK) 1990
Reprinted three times

Text copyright © Cathy Hopkins 1990
Illustrations © Gray Jolliffe 1990

The Author asserts the moral right to
be identified as the author of this work

ISBN 0 00 638355 6

Printed in Great Britain by
HarperCollinsManufacturing Glasgow

CONTENTS

	Introduction	9
1	The Ideal Bait – What Men Think They Want	15
2	Pet Hates – What They Don't Want	21
3	Preparing the Bait – On Looking Good	26
4	The Prey – About Men	35
5	Casting the Hook – How to Get Noticed	44
6	Ploys, Techniques and Trickery	51
7	Biting the Hook – How to Keep Him	61
8	Men and Astrology	75
9	Men and Sex	80
10	Infidelity	87
11	Letting Go	92

'A man without a woman
is like a neck without a pain'
Grafitti

INTRODUCTION

Why Man Hunting?

Well, according to the dictionary definition to hunt means: to pursue wild animals for food or sport.

And man means: human being
                   adult human male (!?)
                   individual person
                   husband (hold on a minute!)
                   manservant/valet (now you're talking)

Hence man hunting. That makes sense doesn't it?

But why do men have to be hunted in the first place? Why go in for the kill when they're already lying there dead at your feet?

The answer is fairly simple but it's amazing how few of us have ever figured it out. Maybe we think that by owning up to what should be self-evident we'll go right off the idea of men because they're such horrors.

Firstly males (at least the ones we're interested in) desperately want sex with women. They have a microchip inserted in their brain that tells them almost from birth to get an erection and to bed as many females as they can in the time they've got. This is primitive man.

As man evolved he realised that this isn't really on because among other things he'd get into lots of fights with other males and uninterested females. So society was formed on a strong religious base, with laws and morals, which said one man one woman, or else.

Those were the good old days. A girl wouldn't dream of sleeping with a man before marriage. Men perceived this as a simple problem of supply and demand and knew that to get laid, first they had to get wed. They had to pursue the female, court her, court her parents and march her up the aisle. Then bingo. But no bingo till then with anyone else. Communities were small and gossip was rife. We were all on the straight and narrow.

But now we have a whole different ball game called the permissive society which basically means you can get laid when you want. It's now so easy for a man to get nookie that there's absolutely no percentage in it for him to get married and have kids. Of course, there are still plenty of guys who do want to, but what if they're the dull ugly ones with sweaty armpits and nylon socks? All the handsome, eligible and interesting men are as happy as bulls in a cow field. Why jump in the river for a drink of water is their attitude.

So why do men seem to be scared of women? One reason is they desire us so much that they make fools of themselves in the approach. They've had a rough ride for a few decades: humiliated if they're tough, laughed at if they're helpful. They couldn't win. A lot of them don't know what line to take with girls any more and so have got over-involved with work or taken up flying lessons instead – where they can view women suspiciously from a safe distance.

Also, there's guilt. They can't come to terms with the fact that we want something more than a one-night stand. We want a father for the kids. A family. They want a leg over. There's a big difference.

Man Hunting is about how to overcome that difference, chase the eligible male, bring him into captivity and keep him there of his own free will so he no longer yearns for the wild.

The time is ripe for man hunting, to seek them out of their hiding places and let them know it's safe to play the game again, it's still fun. And once you've caught one for food or sport (according to the dictionary) and he doesn't provide either, you can always let go of him and start again.

1

THE IDEAL BAIT –
WHAT MEN THINK THEY WANT

I like the girls who do
I like the girls who don't
I hate the girl who says she will
And then she says she won't
But the girl that I like best of all
And I think you'll say I'm right
Is the one who says she never has
But looks as though she might
Max Miller

The big question is: just what *do* men want? Girls have had their say (and plenty) of late – books, articles and magazines.

But what of men, who wisely retreated while the female species ranted and raved and demanded satisfaction? What do the men actually want? Strong girls? Kittens? Big, small, triplets (a big favourite)? A good tip if you want to know a particular man's ideals is to meet his mother. Is she a vamp, or is she an ironer? Chances are that's what he'll be looking for. I asked a number of men about their ideals. Here's a sample of their replies:

1) A *Vogue* model with a masters degree in management consultancy who screams the place down when she comes
2) A small girl, about three foot tall, with a large mouth and flat head for putting your drink on
3) A cross between Marie Curie and Jessica Rabbit
4) An all-forgiving Madonna with a great body who doesn't demand too much sex but is always receptive to it
5) Intelligent, streetwise tart with a heart
6) The girl-next-door who just happens to look like a screen goddess and has her own career
7) Wilma Flintstone(?!)
8) Mother/lover/cook/whore/lady/maid/house-keeper/ accountant/chauffeur
9) As long as she's breathing and can stand unassisted
10) All of the above and very, very, rich

There are two types of women:

a) what men want

b) And what men get

You'll notice the strong sexual overtone in these answers. Is this why women went beserk? Is there any hope? For us? For you? For the survival of the species?

Looking at these ideals and then looking at women and their fantasies in general, they don't seem to add up. It could be war, it has been up till now. What I mean is, look at the myths we girls are fed with. Everywhere you look. Take the commercials, when was the last time you got out of a bath to see some hunk and his Porsche gazing up at your window adoringly, or answered the door to 'him' who just happens to live next door and has run out of coffee? More likely to be some elderly gent (or his wife) complaining about the noise, or some spotty oik in bicycle clips wanting to borrow your puncture outfit.

Prince Charmings and knights in shining armour don't just appear. They have to be sought out, inspired, awoken and encouraged.

It's a hard one this (as the actress said to the bishop): how to give him what he wants (a sort of all-forgiving yet independent wonderwoman) and how to get what you want (a Buddha with balls and a Bentley) when it seems never the twain shall meet.

In the meantime let's look at men's list of priorities, whether you can provide them or not is up to you.

1) Good looks
2) Enthusiasm, confidence, independence, intelligence

3) Patience and warmth
4) Cheerfulness
5) A good listening ability
6) Nymphomania
7) Sense of humour

8) Great tits
9) Great ass
10) Total subservience

2

PET HATES –
WHAT THEY DON'T WANT

> 'A lady's imagination is very rapid,
> it jumps from admiration to love,
> from love to matrimony in a moment'
> Mr Darcy (in Pride & Prejudice, Jane Austen)

With a mind full of tall, dark, heroes from Sir Lancelot to Heathcliff it's no wonder women suffer from the This Is The One syndrome (especially when over thirty and the biological clock is ticking away). This can panic women, and absolutely terrify men.

How to know if this is 'THE ONE'

He likes you

He is not poor

He has a nice smile

He can lick his eyebrows

She thinks	She says	He says	He thinks
Hmm. Nice looking man	Stormy day outside	Yeah, I just got soaked	Hmm. She's OK
Yes, very nice. This chance encounter could be IT	Did you? Poor thing. Take your coat off	Thanks	Nice and sympathetic
Yes, nice face, but could he be The One?	Here, I'll put it on the radiator	Thanks. Worked here long?	Mm, I'm picking up signals I could be on here
My dad's just going to love this guy. I wonder if he'd mind a church service	About three years	What's your name? I'm Thomas	Yep. I'm in there
Thomas. We can name our boys Thomas	Amanda. Shall we name our first boy Thomas?	What?!	What?!

This actually happened to one girl I know. He was talking about the weather, she was mentally giving birth to their first child. Men have also been known to suffer from the This Is The One syndrome but they're often happy to let lots of girls audition for the part.

Men can also be very cagey on first encounters. So many times it's been said that girls fall in love faster and get over it faster. Men are more cautious in the beginning, especially now when many of them are unsure of the rules or even if the same game is being played. It's no longer he courts, she resists then finally succumbs. Women have advanced, grown, evolved. Still, it's always best to be nice at first. 'Be yourself' assertiveness weekends are all very well but statements like 'you'd better like me for all of me, my moods, my unshaven legs, the real me, see I've even got stretch marks and I don't care, hah, hah, I am a free spirit', don't go down too well in the beginning.

Be nice, smile, listen, be enthusiastic – you can hit him with the philosophy and the real you later when he's decided if it's a price worth paying.

> 'Cough and the world coughs with you.
> Fart and you stand alone'
> *Trevor Griffiths*

Here are some more of the things men generally would prefer to do without, at least to start with. Women who are:

- smelly
- vulgar
- too competitive
- emotional
- complicated (ever met a girl who wasn't?)

- whingey/whiney
- loud
- depressed
- demanding
- out-of-control drunk

- nagging
- unstable
- domineering
- clingy

Or women who:

Go on about their periods
Are always on a diet
Don't drink
Don't stop talking about their work
Moan about cellulite and other things they hate about their body
Use four letter words (like 'stop' or 'don't' or 'love')

How to dress if you decide to opt out of the game entirely:

← silly black hat
← cropped spiky hair
← no make-up

← man's shirt
← black baggy jacket

← Hippie bag

← black Gaucho pants
← pop socks
← Big black boots.

3

PREPARING THE BAIT
– ON LOOKING GOOD

> 'Venus de Milo shows what'll happen to you
> if you keep biting your nails'
>
> *Noel Coward*

Ever been told by your current man that he likes you because you understand him, you're a good listener, a nice girl? Probably the kind he'd like to take home to mother and leave there while he goes out with Mimi, Fifi or Lolita.

Ever felt you've got about as much sexual charisma as a dead dog? As much presence as a doormat?

This chapter can change all that. It's about how to turn heads as you walk into a room. 'Who is this vision?' they'll cry. Such style, such individuality, such effortless grace' they'll sigh as you stroll down the street dripping danger and allure. Well, maybe . . .

First thing we've got to look at is your attitude.

How do you rate yourself?

1) Blindingly beautiful
2) Potentially blindingly beautiful
3) Average on a good day
4) Overweight, plain, but nice earlobes and a good listener
5) Quasimodo with bi-focals, webbed feet and ingrowing toenails.

Anyone who marked anything except 1) or 2) is *wrong*. Everyone has it in them to look wonderful in their own particular way.

> 'There are no ugly women.
> Only lazy ones'
> *Helena Rubinstein*

Yes, well I suppose it's OK for her to say that – being a multi-millionairess who gets lots of free facials – but she does have a point.

Ninety per cent of looking good and having sex appeal comes from confidence. Self-confidence. Forget the hair-tips, the miracle diet, the silicone lifts; they all have their place but it really comes down to what you think of yourself.

Don't do it for men, or women, do it for you. If you want other people to boost your confidence, it'll never work – it didn't when Joan Rivers asked her husband to restore hers. 'My boobs have gone,' she said, 'my stomach's gone, say something nice about my legs.' He said, 'Blue goes with everything.' And that's about what you can expect.

Some women don't feel like making a superhuman effort to look beautiful and conform to whatever is in vogue. And why should they? But there's a difference between having your own style that suits you and just being lazy.

If you haven't bothered to give yourself time, people will probably take your lead and not give you any of theirs either. How you look after yourself and the clothes you wear can completely alter the way you feel.

> 'It was a blonde, a blonde to make a bishop kick a hole in a stained-glass window'
> *Raymond Chandler*

I bet her hair didn't need washing and her underwear hadn't lost its shape and gone grey.

FEMALE VS. FEMINISM

> 'A woman who strives to be like a man
> lacks ambition'
> *Graffiti*

So just what is a female? I asked myself. This is what the dictionary said:

Female: of the sex that can bear offspring and produce eggs [preferably scrambled with smoked salmon on a Sunday with fresh coffee, the papers and no interruptions]

And

Feminism: advocacy of women's rights on grounds of equality of the sexes [i.e. he has to produce the eggs etc. every alternate Sunday]

It's years now since women burnt their bras and discovered their G-spots. What started as a rather strong and sometimes confused statement for equality has grown and mellowed as women find their own individual ways of expression beyond the stereotype 'feminist'. After years of feeling held down in second place the initial demands may have seemed a little forceful, like a cork coming out of a champagne bottle, and anyone not of the female sex viewed as 'the enemy'.

One well-mannered man I spoke to held a door open for a woman behind him. 'Do that again and I'll kick your head in, chauvinist pig,' she snapped. He never did do it again.

It's no wonder so many men went into hiding. That kind of attitude has left men opposed to 'feminism': the extreme, the radical, the bitter.

The majority of men I spoke to felt they could respect strong women but drew the line at women who wanted to be like men at the expense of their femininity.

Basically men like the female for the scent, the curves, the touch, texture and the temperament, the things which are essentially female.

That seems natural enough.

And now – how to cash in on what you've got.

TIPS FOR FEELING BRILLIANT

1) Forget shopping for bargains. Save up and buy something wonderful in a great fabric. Kashmir or silk always make you feel sensuous. And well-cut clothing is designed to bring out the best in you

2) Keep your hair well cut and clean. The day you think you're not seeing anyone and so put off washing it will be the day you meet someone devastatingly wonderful. It's Murphy's law

3) Wear underwear that fits and looks good. Grey bras and knickers with the elastic gone are one of the all time turn-offs for men, so what is it going to do to your libido? Go through your drawers (literally) and throw out any that are not fit to be seen

4) Keep your breath fresh, especially if you smoke. If while breathing on your nail polish to dry it, the varnish starts to bubble, you know it's time

to see the dentist and his hygienist

5) Pay attention to details, manicure your toenails even in winter. So no-one sees them – you do, or don't you count?

6) Give yourself thoroughly self-indulgent treats. A massage, a facial, a one-night stand with the local hunk. Whatever makes you feel good. If you get used to the idea that you're worth it so will others

7) Look at your posture. Do you slouch when sitting? Hunch when standing or eating? The Alexander technique is excellent for correcting bad posture habits, think Mae West, Marilyn Monroe, Jessica Rabbit. I bet you wouldn't catch them with their chins on their breast, and their breasts on their stomachs

8) Eat healthy food. The old sayings 'beauty comes from within' and 'you are what you eat' are still true. Hair and skin glow on a healthy diet and are dull on a stodgy junk food diet

9) Live a balanced life. Give yourself time off to thoroughly relax and recharge

10) Think positive. Of all the things you wear, your expression is the one that people see first. If you feel miserable and bored with yourself, so will others, so get help and do something about it

Of course there are coverups, make-up, expensive clothes, sunglasses but if you're putting it on to coverup that's exactly what'll come across.

OK, enough of the serious stuff. Let's meet the enemy . . . .

4

THE PREY – ABOUT MEN

> In the garden of Eden lay Adam
> Complacently stroking his madam
> And loud was his mirth
> For on all of the earth
> There were only two balls and he had 'em
>
> *Anon*

It may be a good idea to memorize this verse when out man hunting, for in it lies the key to the male psyche. As the green beret slogan goes 'if you've got 'em by the balls their hearts and minds will follow'.

A man's most delicate parts are known by many names: The family jewels, three-piece suite, meat and two veg, one-eyed milkman (that would make a great name for a rock band. – 'And now introducing The One-Eyed Milkman and his Swinging Kanakas').

To be treated with respect and understanding, these bits are the sail that steer the boat, the star that charts the journey. It points and the man follows, whoever the man, high or low, Moby Dick and his Jingleberries Rule OK.

But first, its not a bad idea to have a clear picture of what type of man you want. Like woman, man can be a great mystery, one minute fickle and inconsistent and the next if fed, watered and treated kindly can be trained into performing the most domestic of tasks, complete with kiss-me-quick apron.

In order to understand the complexity of man's nature it would be helpful to study the chart overleaf where you can see quite clearly the history and development of man from Adam.

Adam had three sons, yes three! Cain and Abel came first, Cain being the original Rambo type (where he got it from is the great mystery, – back in Cain's day there was no TV violence, so what was he all about?). Anyway he murdered Abel who was a bit of a dreamer but basically OK. It really upset his sons, though, and they became the original philosphers because of the tragedy and sat about thinking why and when, and how and where. Cain's descendents, needless to say, were all adventurers and heroes and big bully boys – as you can see from the chart. Seth came later, he was Adam's third son and was a real sweetie who worked hard in the fields and begat a lot of sons from the fruit of his loins. From him came the nice guys, the stamp collectors and the aeroplane model makers.

The chart is on the broad side, more generally men can be divided into two categories. Nice or naughty. If you're really lucky you get one of the latter whose reformed or mellowed or just not as young as he used to be.

THE EVOLUTION OF MAN

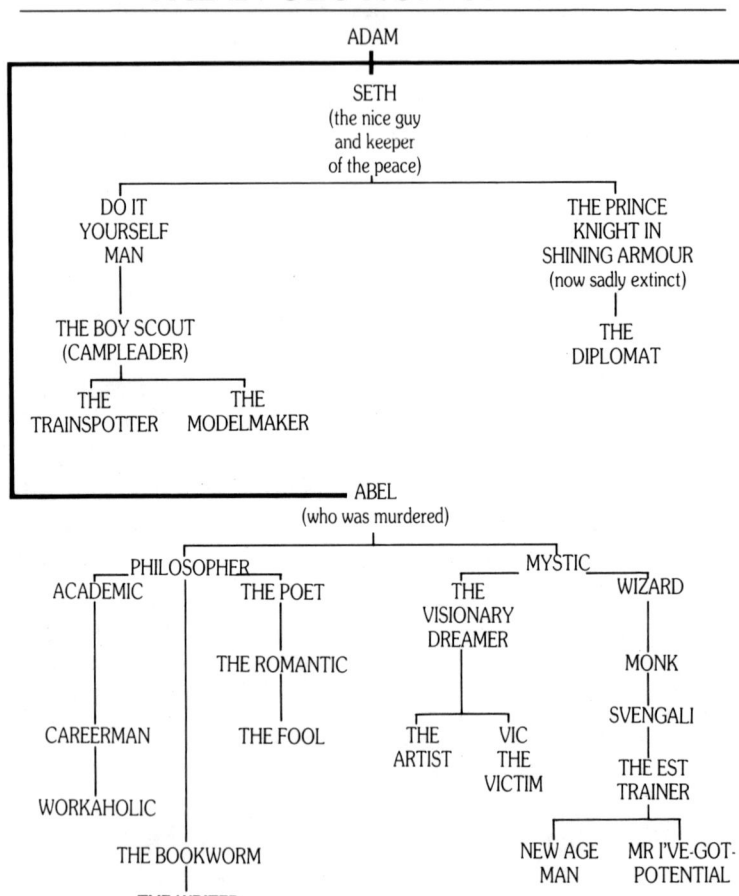

ADAM

SETH
(the nice guy
and keeper
of the peace)

DO IT
YOURSELF
MAN

THE PRINCE
KNIGHT IN
SHINING ARMOUR
(now sadly extinct)

THE BOY SCOUT
(CAMPLEADER)

THE
DIPLOMAT

THE
TRAINSPOTTER

THE
MODELMAKER

ABEL
(who was murdered)

PHILOSOPHER

MYSTIC

ACADEMIC

THE POET

THE
VISIONARY
DREAMER

WIZARD

THE ROMANTIC

MONK

CAREERMAN

THE FOOL

THE
ARTIST

VIC
THE
VICTIM

SVENGALI

WORKAHOLIC

THE EST
TRAINER

THE BOOKWORM

NEW AGE
MAN

MR I'VE-GOT-
POTENTIAL

THE WRITER

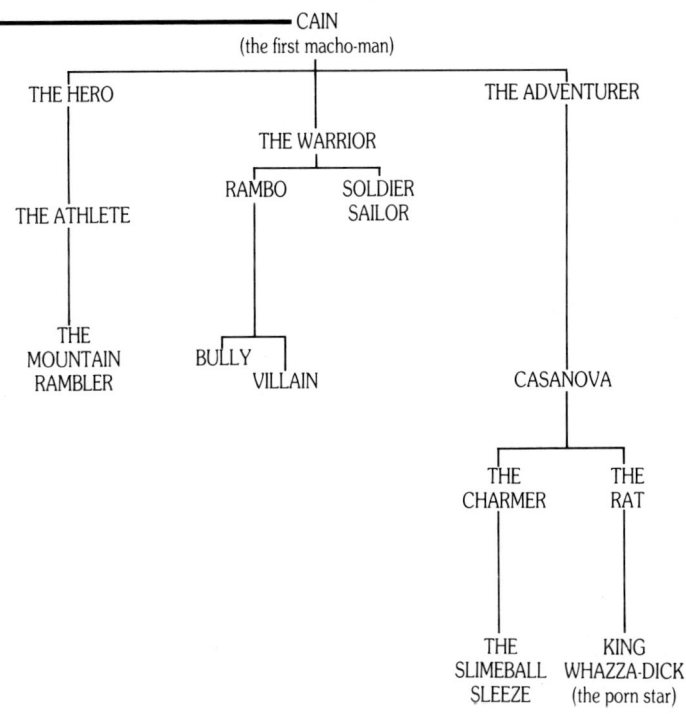

CAIN
(the first macho-man)

THE HERO

THE ADVENTURER

THE WARRIOR

RAMBO

SOLDIER
SAILOR

THE ATHLETE

THE
MOUNTAIN
RAMBLER

BULLY
VILLAIN

CASANOVA

THE
CHARMER

THE
RAT

THE
SLIMEBALL
SLEEZE

KING
WHAZZA-DICK
(the porn star)

HOW TO SPOT . . .

. . . the lurking bastard	. . . the nice guy
mischievous twinkle in the eye, looks straight through your clothes	kindly expression, looks you straight in the eye
disarming smile and perfect teeth	encouraging smile
says sorry, but does it again and won't change	says sorry, doesn't do it again and is willing to change
lies	tells the truth
totally unreliable, but fun if you don't want to get serious	reliable
is charming and dangerous	is charming and safe
unfaithful, amoral, immoral but brilliant at pretending not to be	faithful and loyal
great at getting taxis and getting served in bars. Even better at getting you to do it for him	gets served in the end after all the lurking bastards have pushed in
naughty	nice
you never find out till it's too late	often don't realise till it's too late

A lurking bastard looks like this:

Whereas a nice guy looks more like this:

A few of my friends reckon there's a third category – the wimp. But I reckon there are nice wimps and wimps who'd be lurking bastards if they had enough confidence, so proving my theory yet again. And guys – don't take offence – I'm sure this theory applies to women too!

WHERE TO FIND MEN

Maps don't work, common sense does. Think about what type of man you want and then think about where he's likely to be

Where to find men:

In bars

Beneath contempt

Under the influence

Behind with the payments

Beyond redemption

Over the hill

On your best friend

found. In general you're not going to find a homely academic in a loud disco or the type who likes to party on a donkey trekking holiday in Yorkshire.

Here are some suggestions:

The launderette, supermarket, local gym, sports club, work, parties, night classes, spiritual/religious or political groups, 'growth' workshops, car rallies anywhere

But once you've found him then what?

5

CASTING THE HOOK - HOW TO GET NOTICED

> 'A beauty is a woman you notice.
> A charmer is one who notices you'
> *Adlai Stevenson*

The art of getting noticed is to make sure he notices you've seen him and you noticed him. But what if he's barely given you a second glance, or you met him at a party, he was polite, friendly but didn't pursue you or ask for your number?

Before you wonder if your appeal is fading, could it be?

1) He's married to his work
2) He's married (a wife, a girlfriend)
3) He's involved (possibly with himself)

3(b) He thinks you're stupid.

4) He's had a horrible accident
5) He's got no self-confidence
6) He's gay
7) He's terrified of women

8) He fancies your friend who's been standing behind you flashing her tits
9) He's got a rash on his bum and isn't taking any chances
10) He hasn't got his contact lenses in
11) He has absolutely no taste
12) Hasn't resolved his relationship with his mother

Lots of reasons. Add some of your own. But how do you make an impression, get his attention and inspire him to make what looks like the first move?

Try these:

IMMEDIATE

1) Fall over him
2) Position yourself so he falls over you (great way to start a relationship – him at your feet and apologising)
3) Spill something over him (preferably washable, not hot and only a splash)
4) Block his car in (with a note explaining where you are if he wants to move his car)

5) Position yourself in his eye-line. Make excuses to walk past him
6) Flirt outrageously with someone else

LONGTERM

1) Do your homework: find out all about him from mutual friends then next time you meet him while chatting reveal your knowledge, he'll be astounded at how perceptive you are.
   e.g.
   She: Hi, nice to see you again. We met last week at Mary's
   He: Oh yeah?
   She: You look like the kind of man who never suffers from premature ejaculation
   He: My God! You're so perceptive, give me your phone number immediately!
2) Solicit help, get mutual friends to throw a lunch/dinner and invite both of you
3) Find out where he works. Accidentally bump into him as he's leaving for lunch
4) Find out which gym/supermarket he goes to – again accidental meeting

Find out something about him

Right:

5) Find out his interests and get involved, unless of course his interest happens to be someone called Sara

OTHER WAYS OF GETTING NOTICED

1) Take your clothes off
2) Offer any part of your anatomy and say put this in your mouth honey. Immediately he'll think of mummy and you're a smash hit
3) Show him your stocking and suspendered legs and ask if he approves
4) Make eye contact and lick your lips slowly
5) Follow him into the loo
6) Beckon him over, adjust his tie, even if he hasn't got one on
7) Slither past him and whisper something suggestive in his ear
8) Ask him if he's Norwegian, he's bound to wonder why you asked that

These don't always work but why not take a chance?

6

PLOYS, TECHNIQUES AND TRICKERY

> 'It takes a lot of experience
> for a girl to kiss like a beginner'
> *Ladies Home Journal*

Different approaches work on different men. Once you've assessed the type of man you're hunting you've got to look at what type of approach is going to work best.

1) The 'Be-Yourself' approach (for straightforward men)

As the Greeks say '1000 men can't undress a naked man' (or

woman for that matter) and that is the basis for this technique.

a) Be-yourself
b) Don't try to copy anyone else or walk in anyone else's footsteps
c) The best become the best by being themselves. No one can shake you. If he doesn't like it he wasn't for you anyway

This approach works best in the long run as he's not going to be disappointed later if some phoney act put on to impress him falls through.

2) The 'God-I'm-Impressed-With-You' technique (for most men)

a) Be attentive, fascinated
b) Lots of enthusiastic body language (leaning forward, nodding, exclaiming)

c) Lots of eye contact
d) Laugh at all his jokes, be vastly entertained and impressed

e) Be grateful – let him know he's enlightening you
f) Get into his intimate space but don't touch him – smell his aftershave, brush a hair from his jacket

Flattery gets you everywhere.

3) The 'Mummy-Therapist' technique (for little boys at heart)

a) Make him feel safe and understood
b) Feed him good nutritious food
c) Listen to him
d) Encourage him
e) Get him little treats
f) Don't scold or judge him
g) Only see the best in him

This one can work brilliantly and is very popular worldwide. It can backfire though if not genuine. You can start to resent the fact that what you presented in the first place is what he's grown to expect (and who can blame him!).

4) The 'Doormat' technique (for bossy, bully boys who like women to be seen and not heard)

a) Get an apron with 'welcome, wipe your feet' written on it
b) Always let him have his way
c) Serve his every whim
d) Never complain
e) Tell him he's wonderful at every opportunity
f) Dress exactly the way that pleases him the most, regardless of what you like

This technique works well for men who believe women are a subspecies born to serve them and can only be kept up by women who probably are.

5) The 'Seductress-Femme Fatale' (for women who want a husband, they're just not sure whose)

a) Impeccable presentation
b) Low, soft voice
c) Toss hair back from face
d) Wonderful perfume, red nails, high heels, silk underwear
e) Graceful, dignified walk and posture
f) Perfect the fleeting come-hither look
g) Long, languid body posturing
h) Home in on your target and make him feel special, the centre of attention
i) Lots of double meaning, innuendos. Talk sex without saying any associated words. Extended eye contact
j) Grab his goolies, but not just yet

Make sure you can deliver what you're offering.

6) The 'One-of-the-Lads' technique
(for men who currently don't want a girlfriend)

a) Become good friends
b) Look after him
c) Don't flirt or touch him, even affectionately
d) Be casual, get involved in his interest
e) Win his trust and build his confidence
f) Let him know you don't want anything from him

After a while when he's lulled into feeling safe and you're not after him, he'll jump on you, start to feel good about women again and go off with your sexy friend Jenny because you were never really into having a relationship with him, you were just good friends. Weren't you? . . .

7) The 'Yoo-Hoo-I'm-Anybody's' technique
(for boys who want a quick one)

a) Wear too much make-up. Lots of shiny lip gloss
b) Clothes a little too tight and a little too revealing
c) Lots of heaving breast
d) Make very clear come-ons
e) Lie on the floor legs akimbo with nothing on but the stereo

This can usually get men easily, but often doesn't necessarily keep them. Be clear about what you want if you're going to try it or else you can end up feeling used.

8) The 'Challenge' (for men who don't like it too easy – this requires undisputed sex-appeal)

a) Play hard to get
b) Flirt outrageously but maintain unavailability
c) Be in control. Disagree intelligently and back up your arguments
d) Observe his answers quietly with a look of amused disdain
e) Practise lines like Mae West's 'Come up and see me sometime. Come up Wednesday – that's amateur night'

A lot of men still feel something or someone is worth having only if they have to work for it – so let them. (This technique can be taken further where you compete with him so competently he feels he has to prove his worth, mainly by jumping on you and showing you what's what.)

9) The 'Whoops-I'm-Pregnant' technique (for suckers)

a) Phone him up the week after 'the date' and say, whoops-I'm-pregnant-and-you're-the-father

Bit risky in this day and age as he's likely to think you're a total prat and be very unsympathetic, but it has been known to work in the past and as this is an empirical study in ways of

catching men cannot be excluded. It is however not a technique to be advised, as manipulation of any sort in relationships isn't such a good idea, at least not one that obvious.

10) The 'Black Widow' technique (for men who like to be possessed)

a) Dress in black and cultivate a look of passion, frustration, tragedy and sensuality
b) Smoulder
c) Don't let the man out of your sight
d) Never be satisfied on any level
e) Inspire his total effort to try

This is the kind of woman who if a man agrees to have lunch with her, shouldn't be surprised to find that he's the lunch.

Do not overdo the Black widow technique..

11) The 'Little-Girl-Princess' technique (for men who like to feel big and protective)

a) Let him know you need help (but not with your overdraft), with a plug, your car, a light bulb
b) Perfect the wide-eyed vulnerable innocent look
c) Wear little girlie clothes
d) Learn to wobble your bottom lip as if you're just about to cry if someone doesn't sort it all out soon
e) Let him teach you how to do things but never learn
f) Praise him emphatically
g) Let him tell you things. Ask him why all the sights in Rome and Greece are named after London cinemas. Let him feel important by putting you straight.

This works well for men who like women to be childlike so they can feel fatherly and strong. But once you've won him then what?

7

BITING THE HOOK –
HOW TO KEEP HIM

> 'Most women set out to try and change a man
> and when they have changed him
> they don't like him'
>
> *Marlene Dietrich*

You had a great night, he was great company, you have so much in common. You laughed a lot. He seemed enamoured. It's love. He said he'd call, that was a week ago.

You've got a few choices.

1) Wait for him to call
2) Call him
3) Arrange an 'accidental' meeting and play it by ear from there

'Accidental' meeting

4) Forget him and look for someone else
5) More research – find out where he goes, what he does, arrange to be there surrounded by people all demanding and loving your attention. (You can pay relatives and friends to do this or hire rent-a-crowd)
6) Take control and don't let the situation arise in the first place. Take his number and say you'll call him. Then leave it for a while so he'll be wondering why *you* haven't called him

One man I know went out one Friday with a girl and really liked her and so intended to call the next week. The following Monday she called him: 'Where do I stand? You said you'd call me, what's going on?' She never saw him again. If you *must* call keep it light.

Right

1) Spare theatre ticket. Want to come?
2) Friends are having a party
3) A bunch of us are . . . (the bunch takes the threat out of it)

Wrong

1) I saw you at the party and knew we were meant for each other – when shall I come over?

2) Why haven't you phoned me?
3) When can you meet my parents?
4) Is there someone else?
5) I want you to father my children
6) Sorry I haven't phoned. I've had really bad period cramps and been a bit depressed
7) I haven't been laid in six months and I'm desperate (on second thoughts he may come straight over)

TEST How much have you learnt so far? Is this right or wrong?

After dinner come home and meet mummy and daddy.

Who said right? Go back to Janet and John books

At this point it's probably a good idea to look at what men say and what they actually mean.

DOUBLESPEAK

Commitment	OK, I'll stay the night
I need space at the moment	For all my other girlfriends
I'll give you my work number	I'm married
Let's just see what happens. See how it goes	Back off
My wife doesn't understand me	She understands perfectly, which is why I'm looking for novelty
Would you like a back rub?	I need an excuse to jump on you
You look tired. Why don't we go away for the weekend?	Don't expect to get much sleep. We'll be too busy bonking
Just back off a bit. I need space	I haven't the guts to finish this, but it's over
God, isn't it warm in here?	Would you like to take some clothes off?

Can I sleep on your couch? I'm too tired to drive home	But not so tired, I couldn't go a few rounds with you, given the slightest encouragement
She meant nothing to me, it was only sex	She meant nothing, but the sex meant a lot
It's in my nature	No way am I going to change, like it or leave it
We're both mature adults	If you don't go to bed with me you're being very childish
We can still be friends though	I don't fancy you anymore and this is probably the last time you'll see me
Oh go on, have a double, relax	With luck you won't remember anything
You've missed the last tube. Trust me, I won't try anything.	I'll only try every trick I know

And remember a watched phone never rings.

EXCUSES

Excuses from men often mean thanks but no thanks, but a genuine excuse for cancellation is usually backed up with an alternative arrangement.

The general rule is, if a man is interested you don't have to wonder why he isn't calling you. He's there.

Of course there are exceptions:

1) Shy men
2) Workaholics
3) Casanovas
4) Lazy men

In which case, is he *really* what you want? Trying to change or reform a man can be a lifetime's task and a complete waste of time. As Oscar Wilde said: 'The only way a woman can ever reform a man is by boring him so completely that he loses all possible interest in life'.

The Art of Good Conversation

On the first date

> 'OK, enough of me. Let's talk about you . . .
> what do you think of me?'
> *Bette Midler in* Beaches *after
> talking about herself for ten minutes*

Try this quiz if you want to know how to keep his interest on a
date

On the first date, do you talk about:

a)   His interests
b)   Your interests
c)   World events?

The right answer is (a), unless of course when you ticked (c)
you meant his opinion or interpretation of world events. As
the saying goes – a gossip talks about others, a bore talks
about himself, and a good conversationalist talks about you.
So get him talking and you'll be home and dry.

Of course, this can be very boring for you and is very
submissive and unfeminist. But this book is about how to
catch a man, not how to enlighten or change him. What you

do with him once you've caught him is your business, but the early days with these creatures are sensitive times and, as on most hunts, a number of facts should be taken into account. Take a few pointers from watching David Attenborough:

Don't	Do
1) Frighten or alarm your prey	1) Get him to trust you
2) Make sudden movements (like jumping on him)	2) Imitate his body language so he feels your empathy with him
3) Don't make loud noises (like doing your Swiss yodelling act – he may feel threatened)	3) Be quiet and peaceful so he knows you're not going to hurt him . . . yet

Don't challenge him until he knows you're friendly, this can take anything from five minutes to five years depending on how evolved he is. Some men are wise old souls, probably having been women in previous incarnations and for some men, bless 'em, it's their first time on the planet and they don't know what's hit them. Being alive is one thing but having to deal with women emerging as individuals in their own right is enough to send their particular evolutionary process into retrogression. Being a tree, a frog or a duck was much easier, at least the enemy was more clearly defined.

How to get a second date:

1) Look interested, fascinated even
2) Laugh in appropriate places
3) Nod encouragingly
4) Spot his obsessions and ask leading questions
5) Study the Bluffers Guide to Good Conversation on the next page

How to make sure you don't get a second date:

1) Yawn while he's telling you his most entertaining story, like the one about when he substituted chilli puree in his friend's haemorrhoid ointment tube
2) Laugh in inappropriate places (like when he's opening up and telling you about how his pet hamster, who was his only friend, mistakenly got put in the spindryer)
3) Look around the room, pointing and winking at other men
4) Fall asleep
5) Start doing animal farmyard impersonations to liven things up

THE BLUFFER'S GUIDE
TO GOOD CONVERSATION

The ground rules:

1) When you can, bluff it
2) When you can't, don't be afraid to say you don't know
3) Remember it only works in the short term. If you're really interested in a particular man in the long run you have to be honest or do some homework
4) Practise until perfect the kind of facial expression that says you know exactly what he's talking about (a sort of cross between constipation and glee)
5) Study your subject and start off with a few general openers that will reveal his areas of interest. E.g.: What do you like to do in your spare time? Do you like to read? What sort of books? etc
6) Learn how to feed him the lines that will get him started on his favourite topics or his pet subjects – if you think he's worth it

Examples:

Right

For the man interested in art

You   I really like the __ movement, though I never really understood the reaction to them in their own time. Why do you think it was?

He   1/4 hr. lecture

You   Mm. Fascinating. And how do you think the work stands up today?

He   1/4 hr. lecture

You   Exactly

He   How wonderful to find someone who feels the same way I do about all this

For the man interested in politics

You   The situation in (Ireland, Beirut, South America, Brent) is very complex. What are your views on the matter?

He   1/4 hr. lecture

You   That's a very interesting outlook. How did you arrive at it?

He   1/4 hr. lecture

You   Do you think there is a solution?

He   1/4 hr. lecture

You   Exactly

He   (*thinks*) What a well-informed woman

Wrong

He   What do you think about —?

You   I don't know anything about it. Bores me silly in fact. Can I have another Malibu cocktail, with a little umbrella in it. I collect them

He   Isn't it awful about —? The headlines were quite shocking this morning

You   You what? I never read the paper

He   . . . world peace is threatened

You   Really? Still you can't always believe what you read, can you? Did you see 'Eastenders' last night. It was great. Johnny committed suicide

Or again maybe you're the highbrow and he watches 'Eastenders', but he's got the cutest butt, you're going through a toy-boy phase so who cares about his IQ

Right

He   Did you see 'Eastenders' tonight?

You   Oh no! I missed it. Fill me in right away on what happened

He   1/4 hr. lecture

You   Gosh! I must get my video fixed, so I don't miss any more. What do you think the outcome will be?

He   1/4 hr. lecture

You   Exactly. You should write TV scripts with your insight

He   (*thinks*) Here's a girl who really shares my interests

You get the idea. It's easy and if you don't know much about a particular subject you probably will by the time you go home.

This technique of bluffing is appallingly manipulative, deceptive and submissive. It also really, really works . . . .

8

MEN AND ASTROLOGY

For a few more clues to your particular man's whims and weak spots, try asking him his sun-sign to see what more can be revealed.

Sign	Key Word	His Ideal
Mr Aries	Energy	Passionate, vital, powerful, a girl who can stand up to him and be his equal on all levels from bedroom to the boardroom
Mr Taurus	Stability	A loyal, sensuous beauty who doesn't play games and just happens to be a gourmet cook and a nymphomaniac
Mr Gemini	Flirtatious	A girl who can floor him with her witty one-liners and keep him well-

		entertained both physically and mentally while he's down there
Mr Cancer	Security	A supportive, homely kind of girl who'll cherish him and yet give him the space he needs for his crabby moods
Mr Leo	Ego	A real glamourpuss needed here. A girl who'll improve his self-image with her blazing sex appeal and charisma
Mr Virgo	Perfection	A female Dr Spock. Intelligent, emotionally calm and tidy, who shares his love of the smell of disinfectant. Cleanliness is a big must
Mr Libra	Beauty	With Venus as his ruler any girl who takes her chance with him would have to have an innate sense of harmony and romance, as well as good looks. Libra hates squalor or bad taste
Mr Scorpio	Magnetism	The way to his heart is to intrigue and bewitch him. Then meet him with passion and sexuality to match his own
Mr Sagittarius	Freedom	He wants a girl who shares his love of space, adventure, excitement and spontaneity. He's not one to be caged in or tied down
Mr Capricorn	Conscientious	A responsible girl with her own status and ambitions and who admires him for his

| Mr Aquarius | Friendship | A girl who will fascinate him with her knowledge and experience. A companion with whom to roam uncharted territory |
| Mr Pisces | Mystical | A sensitive girl with dreamy eyes and her head in the stars who shares the same romantic fantasy as he does |

And if you're wondering just what you can expect from him, imagine this simple scenario and look at all the different ways he could interact in it depending on his star-sign. The evening was fun, you invite him in for a cup of coffee . . . .

His idea

Aries   More like a good excuse to make wild, impetuous love on the floor

Taurus   I hope it won't just be coffee, and I hope it's real coffee not instant, with a little savoury smoked salmon snack, then some dark Swiss chocolates to follow and then who knows where the evening'll lead . . . .

Gemini   Coffee? I'll get a few more bottles of champagne in case her flatmate's in, some good sparky conversation until 3am, then let's see which one's still awake . . . .

Cancer   Coffee and maybe some toasted muffins – a nice homely way to end an evening curled up on the sofa. Maybe we could look through her family photo albums as well

Leo	Coffee. Yes, and I'll make it. It'll be a good excuse to impress the pants off her by showing her I know how to make it the way Rudolf Valentino made his. Strong and spicy – just like me
Virgo	Coffee. Only if it's Columbian medium roasted and I'll only drink it if the cups are clean. I hate stained or chipped cups
Libra	Not sure whether to have coffee or tea, my place or hers. My coffee would be served in elegant art deco bone china as we both sit in exquisite long silk kimonos listening to something serene and sultry. Then we'd probably play out the Kamasutra. (Libran men are the worst playboys of the zodiac)
Scorpio	Coffee. OK, a black one, while she disappears to slip into something more comfortable like her spiderwoman outfit with the black mask and thigh-length leather boots
Sagittarius	I've a better idea. Why go in? Let's get on the back of my bike and roar off into the night and howl at the moon or something equally wild, we can catch a cup on the way back
Capricorn	A good excuse to assess her flat for style, taste and assets. But coffee, no, I'll have tea as I must get a good night's sleep, I've got an early business meeting
Aquarius	Great, now's my chance to find out her theories on the space-time continuum and if she believes in life on other planets
Pisces	Coffee. Yes, out on the balcony overlooking the city gazing up at the new moon. I might even recite my poem to her

Watch out for ambiguity :

9

MEN AND SEX

> *She:* I've heard all about your lovemaking
> *He:* Oh, it's nothing
> *She:* That's what I heard
> *'Rowan and Martins Laugh-in', 1969*

Most men are open to being seduced, but more often than not they'll make the first move. What women can do is make it clear when this is welcome. Let him know what you want and how . . . .

What they like:

> There was a young man from Dumfries
> Who said to his girl, 'If you please
> It would give me great bliss
> If while playing with this
> You would pay some attention to these'

1) They like to know that someone's there with them – they like a response

A man I heard about had an unresponsive girlfriend and complained about her silence. 'Why don't you moan a bit?' he asked. 'Moan?' she said, 'OK!' Next time they were in bed and he's on the vinegar strokes she remembered what he'd said and started moaning: 'I came out of Sainsbury's today and had to stand at the bus stop in the rain for half an hour. No buses, then ten came altogether and not one was a number 12!')

2) The visual. Women who scurry into bed then turn the lights off don't score many points
3) Affection – ask him what pleases him
4) Nice smells. Nice textures. Silk, satin
5) Surprise/spontaneity
6) Enthusiasm and exclamations (E.g. 'Wow, that's enormous' – you can practise the degree of

surprise and sincerity at home in front of the
mirror)
7)   Find out his fantasies and fetishes

8) Pretty underwear. Most men from nine to ninety are turned on by stockings and suspenders, lace and silk – the works

And there's always a few things you shouldn't do:

1) Kiss like you're trying to clean the drains
2) Watch TV over his shoulder while he's doing his best moves
3) Get up and immediately have a wash after sex
4) Tell him that although your last lover was bigger it really doesn't matter because size doesn't count and it's what you do with it and . . . . Don't be surprised if he disappears and doesn't come back
5) Fart or throw up
6) Laugh at him or any part of his anatomy
7) Give him a score in comparison to your ex-lovers
8) Give route directions
9) Shout the wrong name
10) Use sharp teeth during oral sex
11) Do a screaming performance in too public a place – like at his parents' house
12) Keep demanding more (Allow for the three ages of man: tri-weekly, try-weekly, try-weakly)
13) Be dishonest and fake orgasm (Men never fake erections)
14) Just as he's getting excited, light up a cigarette

One man I spoke to admitted that after years of thinking he was the world's greatest lover and really knew how to handle women he finally realised he never really knew if he'd satisfied any of them. Please, he said, if you put anything about sex in your book ask women to be directive. Ask them:

a) to take responsibility for your own pleasure or lack of it
b) to tell men explicitly what pleases or displeases at the appropriate time. (Not just after sex – 'Yuk, that was awful, you should have done it this way')
c) while giving directions be sure to give praise and encouragement where it's due, or you could deflate him totally in more ways than one
d) keep communicating as moods and feelings change

He admitted that this can be difficult because many women recognize how touchy the male ego can be when it comes to sexual prowess and so they keep quiet – no man likes to think he doesn't know what to do. But many of them don't, and unless a woman teaches them never will. So girls, it's up to you to tell them what you want, but be subtle.

'My father told me all about the birds
and the bees – the liar.
I went steady with a woodpecker until I was twenty-one'
Bob Hope

Here are a few tips though on what not to say:

1) You mean that isn't your finger?
2) That looks like a penis only smaller
3) Is it in yet?
4) My last boyfriend . . .
5) Not yet, not yet (if this goes on for hours)
6) Hurry up and come, 'Dallas' is on in five minutes

Just about every man I spoke to said that they absolutely cannot stand women talking about their ex's as they can't bear to think any other man has been as close as they have. As Edward Dahlberg said, 'What most men want is a virgin who's a whore' – you're supposed to know all there is to know about lovemaking but never have done it with anyone.

10

INFIDELITY

> 'I told my wife I was seeing a psychiatrist.
> Then she told me that she was seeing a psychiatrist,
> a plumber and a bartender'
>
> *Roger Dagenfield*

One of the things many women fear most is infidelity, but just what are the tell-tale signs?

Definite:

He gets a sexual disease that you definitely haven't got

Maybe:

1) Someone keeps phoning and hanging up when you answer
2) He's on the phone and hangs up when you walk in
3) He's distant and secretive
4) He's incredibly nice, extra attentive and brings you flowers out of the blue
5) Comes in late and often works late
6) Looks awkward when you look at him directly
7) Twitching feet. (According to Diana Dors a liar can control all parts of his body except his feet)
8) Lipstick marks and smell of perfume (not yours)
9) New trendy underwear/boxer shorts
10) Renewed interest in his appearance
11) Obvious new influence in dress sense and style
    (He 1: How long have you been wearing a bra?
    He 2: Ever since my wife found it in the car)

This list is a bit ambiguous since all these signs could be just what they are with no deception behind them. On the other hand you may be the last to find out, like the female chat-show host who asked Joan Collins who the best man she'd ever had was: 'your husband', she replied.

If you have been badly let down by some rat who lied to you and betrayed you, you can either take it lying down or get

The tights? Ah..yes...well I always keep a pair in the car in casethe fan belt goes
I see. And what about the panties and the vibrator?

even. ('Heaven has no rage like love to hatred turned. Nor hell a fury, like a woman scorned' – William Congreve)

Just thinking about doing any of the following will make you feel better. It won't bring him back, and if you did any of them you'd probably end up in court. But imagine his expression if . . . .

1) You wrote a bestseller about you and him with detailed accounts of all pervy things he liked doing
2) Put sugar in his petrol tank
3) Sent all his love letters/personal photos to his new girlfriend
4) Dialled the time in Hong Kong on his phone and left the phone off the hook
5) When he's away, got into his flat, covered his carpet and settee with alfalfa sprouts then watered them. There should be a nice healthy growth when he gets back
6) Hired a huge advertising poster with 'Jeremy's got a small one' written on it
7) Cut the crotch out of all his trousers
8) Sewed up the ankles and wrists of all his clothes so he can't get his legs or arms in
9) Shouted across a crowded room that you'd always faked it
10) Told his parents he's gay

11) You saw him with his new girl and asked 'My God Nigel, I thought I was seeing you on Thursday. What are you doing here?' and *who* is this??' (He'll have a fine time explaining that away)
12) Told him you wish you'd known him while he was alive
13) Sold your story to the *Sport*

Well, a girl can dream. Maybe there are other ways of recovering besides seeking revenge. . . .

Or wait till you know he's out of his office, and do this :

Oh Hello - is that Mr Dobley's secretary? This is the clinic can you ask him to call us - the tests unfortunately proved positive and we need to trace all his contacts over the last five years.

11

LETTING GO

> 'My Oberon, what visions have I seen.
> Me thoughts I was enamoured of an ass'
> *Shakespeare*

Parting is never easy as it often involves one of two people feeling rejected. You or him. The best advice is make it quick and with any luck, like Titania in *A Midsummer Night's Dream*, you will look back and wonder what you ever saw in him.

But if you don't feel like that and you simply feel terrible then you've got a few choices:

      1)   Get philosophical (all part of life's rich tapestry,

everything changes, etc)

2) Get angry (the shit, the bastard, the rat, etc)
3) Get upset (God!, how I loved him, there'll never be another like him . . .)
4) Eat (chocolate, chips, cake – who needs men as long as they make American toffee and pecan icecream?)
5) Go shopping (but there's no-one to appreciate my new red high heels)
6) Get drunk (who cares anyway, not me . . .)
7) Rediscover your girlfriends and discover they're all married and you're a threat to them
8) Get over it (sure!)
9) Start reading books on relationships again (e.g.: 'The Shite Report on Men', 'Daft Women, Daft Choices', etc)
10) Take up night classes (pottery, car mechanics, Urdu)
11) Get into counselling (now just where did I, we, my parents, teachers and unborn children go wrong? Finally discover it was when you found out there was no Santa, you've never trusted again and keep creating the same pattern of loss)
12) Take a vow of celibacy (when you ain't got nothing, you got nothing to lose)
13) Find someone else (so much for vows!)
14) Decide never to say never

Most women go through one or all of the choices in the end, but in different orders.

Maybe you still like the guy, it just wasn't working for you. You don't want to hurt his feelings, so tell him in private then he'll have time to fabricate his side of the story before it goes public. Remember, though, if you've met someone else and decide to tell your soon-to-be-ex the truth, the chances are some strange rumours are going to circulate in the gym about you (she was a dyke, money-grabber, bitch, frigid, possessive . . .) so give him something to tell the boys and save his face and your reputation.

1) You need space to find yourself
2) You're off to find God and enlightenment
3) You're going to live in another area
4) You're mixed up and he deserves better (chances are he'll believe this!)

But if the guy is a rat and you hated him, go back to Chapter 10.

Don't:

1) Beg or call him to come back
2) Whine or cry
3) Get bitter, it eats you up in the end
4) Use any form of emotional blackmail to keep him

Do cry, grieve, get angry, release it all. Don't hang on, look at what happened and learn from it. Life goes on, the game's still played, the hunt continues.

Please find listed below more humour titles available from HarperCollins:

French For Cats	Henry Beard	0 00 637823 4	£4.99
Advanced French for Exceptional Cats	Henry Beard	0 00 638078 6	£5.99
Official Exceptions to the Rules of Golf	Henry Bead	0 58621843 2	£6.99
The Official Politically Correct Dictionary	Henry Beard	0 586 21726 6	£4.99
Girl Chasing	Cathy Hopkins	0 00 637940 0	£4.50
Keeping It Up	Cathy Hopkins	0 00 637855 2	£4.99
Merde!	Geneviève	0 00 637793 9	£5.99
Merde Encore!	Geneviève	0 00 637785 8	£5.99
Wicked French	Howard Tomb	0 207 16665 X	£2.99
Wicked Italian	Howard Tomb	0 207 16666 8	£2.99
World's Best Business Jokes	Charles Alverson	0 207 16385 5	£2.99
World's Best Drinking Jokes	Ernest Forbes	0 207 16607 2	£3.50
World's Best Marriage Jokes	Ernest Forbes	0 00 637839 0	£3.50
More Golf Jokes	Ernest Forbes	0 00 637934 6	£3.50
World's Best Dirty Limericks	Harold H Hart	0 207 14650 0	£2.99
World's Best Irish Jokes	Des Machale	0 207 14836 8	£2.99
More World's Best Irish Jokes	Des Machale	0 207 15069 9	£2.99
Still More of the World's Best Irish Jokes	Des Machale	0 207 16880 6	£2.99
World's Best Scottish Jokes	Des Machale	0 207 15805 3	£2.99
World's Best Golf Jokes	Robert McCune	0 00 637802 1	£2.99
More of the World's Best Dirty Jokes	Mr J	0 207 14231 9	£2.99
Still More of the World's Best Dirty Jokes	Mr J	0 207 14730 2	£2.99
More World's Best Drinking Jokes	Edward Phillips	0 00 637959 1	£2.99